Fun STEM Challenges

BUILDING MARBLE RUNS

by Marne Ventura

PEBBLE
a capstone imprint

Pebble Plus is published by Pebble, an imprint of Capstone.
1710 Roe Crest Drive, North Mankato, Minnesota 56003
www.capstonepub.com

Library of Congress Cataloging-in-Publication data is available on the Library of Congress website.
ISBN: 978-1-9771-1300-9 (library binding)
ISBN: 978-1-9771-1780-9 (paperback)
ISBN: 978-1-9771-1306-1 (ebook pdf)

Summary: Describes how to build marble runs using cardboard tubes and paper plates.

Image Credits
Photographs by Capstone: Karon Dubke;
Marcy Morin and Sarah Schuette, project production;
Heidi Thompson, art director

Alamy: MBI, 7, Newscom: dpa/picture-alliance/Jan Woitas, 5, Shutterstock: Hulshof Pictures, 1

All the rest of the images are credited to: Capstone Studio/Karon Dubke

Editorial Credits
Erika L. Shores, editor; Juliette Peters, designer;
Eric Gohl, media researcher;
Laura Manthe, production specialist

All internet sites appearing in back matter were available and accurate when this book was sent to press.

Capstone thanks Darsa Donelan, Ph.D., assistant professor of physics, Gustavus Adolphus College, St. Peter, MN, for her expertise in reviewing this book.

Printed in China.
2493

Table of Contents

What Is a Marble Run?

A marble run is a ramp.

One end is high.

The other end is low.

Marbles roll down the run.

Why Build Marble Runs?

Marble runs are tiny roller coasters.

We use them to make marbles move.

By changing the run, we can change the way marbles move.

Make Your Own

You can make a marble run with cardboard tubes and paper plates. Find large and small marbles and a big piece of cardboard too. What else can you use to make a marble run?

Cut the tubes in half the long way.

Put them together to make one long tube.

Lean it on some stairs. What happens
when you set a marble at the top?

Gravity pulls the marble down.

Lean your marble run on

a high table. Does the marble

roll fast or slow? Try a low table.

Does the marble go faster

or slower?

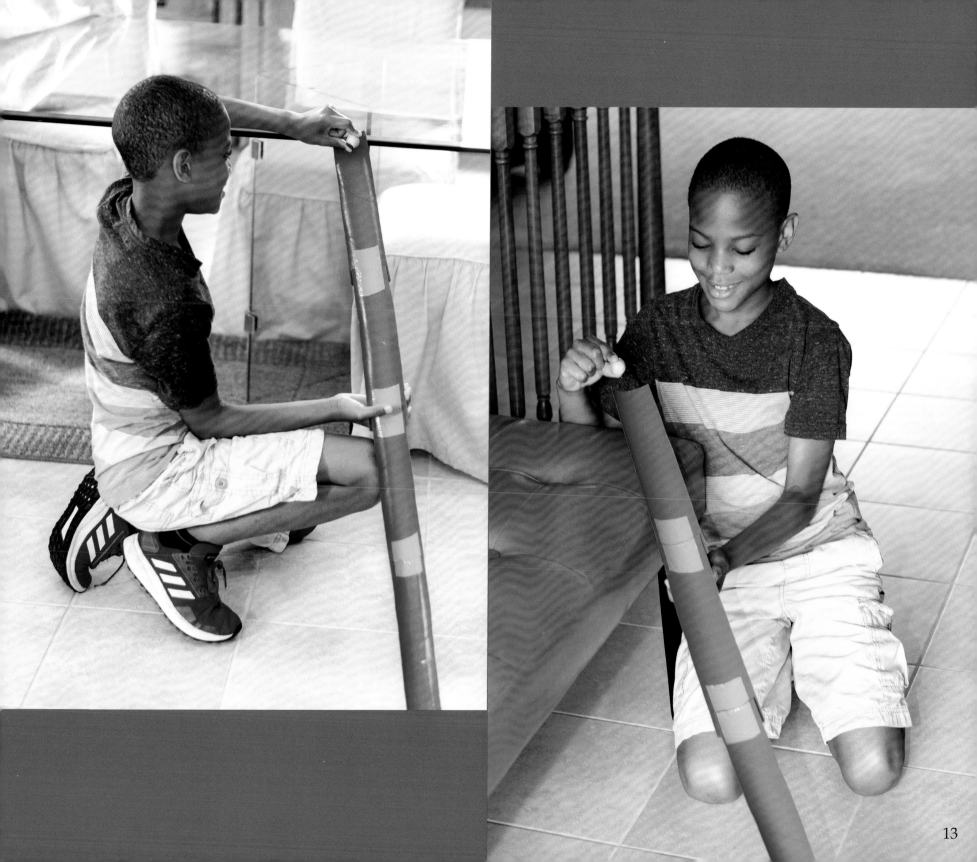

Tape some uncut tubes to the cardboard.

Do the marbles move from one tube

to the next? What changes do you

need to make? Do the tubes need

to be closer together or farther apart?

Cut some tubes in half the long way.

Tape them to the cardboard.

How can you make the
marble move down?

How can you make it turn?

Cut the rims from four paper plates.
Tape them together. Tape them
on cardboard tubes. Can you
make a marble roll down?
Does it stay on the loop?

What Did You Learn?

Gravity pulls marbles down. A marble will roll faster down a high hill. Marble runs can make marbles turn or loop.

Glossary

drop—to fall

gravity—the downward pull of the earth

loop—a curved shape

ramp—a track that goes from high to low

roll—to move by turning like a ball

run—a ramp

smooth—not bumpy

turn—to move in a new direction

Read More

Chin, Jason. *Gravity*. New York: Roaring Press Books, 2014.

Mckenzie, Precious. *Roller Coasters*. Vero Beach, FL::
Rourke Educational Media, 2016.

Rice, Dona Herweck. *Creative Machines*. Huntington Beach, CA:
Teacher Created Materials, Inc., 2019.

Internet Sites

Roller Coaster Facts for Kids
https://kids.kiddle.co/Roller_coaster

Tinker Lab
https://tinkerlab.com/toilet-paper-roll-marble-run/

Critical Thinking Questions

1. What else can you use to make a marble run?

2. How is a marble run like a ramp?

3. What makes marbles roll down a run?

Index